SIS, YOU ARE THE UNIVERSE: WORDS OF ENCOURAGEMENT, HEALING, AND LOVE FOR BLACK WOMEN

○

PHYLICIA FRENCH

Sis, You Are The Universe: Words of Encouragement, Healing, and Love for Black Women by Phylicia French

Published by Mission Mantra Media

ISBN: 978-1-7369545-0-8

Acknowledgments

I would like to acknowledge my amazing team of professionals that contributed to the creation of *Sis, You Are the Universe*. I thank each and every one of you for your professionalism, fantastic work, dedication, and support.

Editor • Jo Palmer
Instagram • @jpalm126

Illustrator • Alaa Ali
www.artbyalaa.com
Instagram • @artbyalaaa

Book Designer • Rose Zinnia
www.rosezinnia.earth
Instagram • @rosie.zinnia

Author Headshot Credit

Photographer and Makeup Artist • Crystal Vonshaè
Instagram • @crystal_vonshae_
Facebook • Crystal Vonshaè

Hair • Dion Jackson

Nails • Nail Khemistry by Kay
Instagram • @nailkhemistry
Facebook • Nail Khemistry by Kay

This book is dedicated to my beautiful mother, Phyllis French. I am eternally grateful for all that you have done for me. I do not believe there is a word in the English language that can describe all that you are. Thank you for showing me love that knows no limits. Thank you for the many sacrifices you made for me to be the woman I am today. Thank you for showing me hard work and dedication, but more than anything, the importance of love and family. You had a full time job and went to school, but made sure to show up for sports, cheerleading, dance performances, and to go off on teachers when they mistreated your baby. Thank you for allowing me to be myself and loving me for all that I am. I thank God for choosing you to be my mother. I love you forever and always, my amazing mommy.

You are
magical !

With love,

Phylicia
Taneh

FORWARD

I want to start by saying this is not a "self-help" book. In fact, I even hate (yes, I know this is a strong word) that word. One of the definitions of self-help is to receive help without the assistance of others. Everyone needs someone and we cannot improve or transform into our best selves on our own. Self-help has also become so commercialized and whitewashed—it is not for me. Now listen, I still have to play the game, so you may see this book in the self-help section of wherever you find this—don't judge me.

This is a book to encourage, inspire, and spread love to my beautiful black sisters. These words of encouragement, healing, and love are going to validate and confirm things you already know in your soul. Each page in this book has its own energy. When you read these words, think about how you want to or have already applied them to your life, and pay attention to your body and energy. This book can be a tool to help you remove barriers that prevent you from accessing your definition of your best self. I hate books that make you feel like the work you have to do to heal, exist, transform, or level up is simple, because it is not; but I wholeheartedly believe you can do it.

I have had many trials and tribulations and I do not claim to have it all figured. I am on a journey to become my definition of the best Phylicia. I have days where I feel on top of the world and days where I need encouragement and love to make it through. With the wisdom I have gained through my experiences, my divine gift to motivate and inspire, and love and advice from the amazing community of black women in my life, I give you this book of love to encourage and uplift you, Queen. May the words you read connect with your spirit and confirm the magic you possess within. You are the universe!

PART 1: WORDS TO ENCOURAGE, MOTIVATE, AND HEAL BLACK WOMEN

SIS, YOU ARE THE UNIVERSE

There are people in your life who seek to undermine your value.
They offer you the breeze,
so you ask for something greater—strong winds.
They offer you lakes,
so you ask for something greater—oceans.
They offer you hills,
so you ask for something greater—mountains.

They will grant your requests and present their strong winds, oceans,
and mountains in way that makes you feel so valued.
Guess what, sis? You still deserve more, and they know it!

You know why you can demand the highest winds in the solar
system on Neptune? The largest ocean in the solar system on
Jupiter? The largest structures in the universe—superclusters?
Because you, your excellence, your worth, and your value expands
beyond the beyond.

You, my dear, are planets, space,
energy, time, galaxies, and light.
You, my dear, are the universe!
Demand what you are truly worth!

THE REIMAGINED STRONG BLACK WOMAN

The narrative of the strong black woman is true,
but it's a slippery slope.
We are the mother of civilization, yet in the same breath,
the most disrespected and abused.
Carrying the title of "strong black woman" comes with unrealistic
expectations and can be a heavy burden to bear.
We suffer because society assumes our strength means we are
bulletproof, and our power is used against us.

You are not strong just because of what you can endure without
crumbling, your ability to shake things off, or "pushing through."
It is important to reimagine what it means to be a strong black
woman even if the rest of the world refuses.

We are powerful, but we experience pain.
We are victorious, but we are vulnerable.
We are heroes, but we need space to heal.
We are resilient, but we are, at times, fragile.

We may seem to possess the power of a superhuman, because
of our ability to carry the weight of the world on our shoulders
without falter, but we are not immune to the human experience.
Being a strong black woman does not strip you of your right to
show your vulnerability.
And even if no one else acknowledges that fact,
you should make it your business to.

HUMBLE WHERE?

Do not let humility step in the way of owning your greatness.
Sometimes you need to toot your own horn,
but being perceived as arrogant
prevents you from doing so.

You have worked so hard for all you have,
you are magical, and you continue to kick ass.
Why do you have to be modest about this?
Today is the day you tell Kendrick Lamar, "fuck being humble and
sitting down."

You are going to rise as high as a giant,
put on your crown,
be the baddie you truly are, and
make sure every person, in your presence,
knows you are royalty.

DESTROYING THE BOX

Most of us have been encouraged to think
outside the box at some point.
The box is a confined space,
filled with limitations and barriers,
so, you are encouraged to go beyond
the box's limitations and standards.

The concept of the box is problematic because
it exists as a point of reference
EVEN when you're thinking outside of it.
This means you are not truly free in thought.

Queen, destroy that damn box!
When the box is completely destroyed, you give yourself full
freedom to exist, create, feel, and be, in a way that knows no
boundaries or restrictions.
Thinking and being without parameters unlocks so much
creativity.

Free yourself from limitations!
There are no restrictions when the box doesn't exist.

MYTHS OF INCONSISTENCY

Queen, you are not inconsistent,
you are healing.
You get going, then life knocks you down.
You don't feel you have the luxury of time to regroup,
so you want to quickly get back up.
Once you get going, life knocks you down again.
You beat yourself up because you refer to your healing
as inconsistency.
Change your language and
you will change the way you view your progress.
You must have a solid foundation of healing before you can
get up, walk, run, and fly.
Remember, healing is healing and
not synonymous with inconsistency.
Think of this time as progress to get back to
what you are working for.

SHOW OUT

If the "I'm gonna show them" mindset gets you motivated to make moves, then take that motivation and move forward.

But, "they" aren't buying tickets to your show
no matter how amazing it is
because they don't want to see you shine.

Do it for you!
Show YOU and show OUT for you!

LINE LEADERS

Society tries to put black women in the back of the line, but we refuse to stay there.
Sure, we may start off in the back of THEIR line, but we boss up, turn around, and lead our OWN lines.

We create opportunities and spaces
for black women to excel within our lines.
Our lines lead us into prosperity—
To a place where we can understand our magic and value.
To a place where we can achieve peace and enjoy the fruits of our labor.

We change our circumstances by changing our perspectives.

RESTING IN WRONG

You know when something is wrong.
It doesn't feel right, you feel off,
but you ignore it and stay in it anyway?

Your divine energy will not allow you
to fully rest in wrong.
You have this feeling in the pit of your stomach
that will not go away.
Explore it, trust it, feel it, say it aloud.
Whether you stop resting in wrong today or two years from now,
eventually, you will say enough is enough.

Do not be the author of a redemption story that did not have to exist.

MOTHER TIME

20/20 hindsight lives in the present,
not the past you have figured out and wish you could change.
Work on your past self, but be fair to you,
you did not know then what you know now.
You will continue to remain in a cycle of working on your past and
worrying about your future,
if you neglect your present.
The today you ignore becomes
the past you have to work out and explore.
Society is structured so our lives are mostly focused on
surviving and thriving for our future selves.
This often prevents your present self from
enjoying the beauties of life.
Find coping mechanisms
to reduce the pressures of living for your future.
Living in the yesterdays and tomorrows takes away
from the gift of now.

SELF-LOVE

When you truly love yourself above all,
you are clear on the ways you love
and the ways in which you need to receive love.

Self-love can help you heal the deepest wounds.
Self-love can be the key to unlock your greatest potential.
Self-love can be your compass as you navigate life.
Self-love is a personal journey that looks different for everyone.

Don't know where to start?
Think about the people or things you love in your life.
What does that love look like?
What makes you love them/it?
How does it make you feel?

Step outside of yourself
and think about who you are
and how you could love you,
then work on ways to apply that love to yourself.
The greatest love of all is loving you.

LEMON

Life gave you a lemon
and you made lemonade, lemon zest,
lemon sugar, and lemon pepper.
Queen, you are phenomenal!

ROLLERCOASTER OF LIFE

Rollercoasters have many ups and downs,
twists and turns, can be frightening, yet exhilarating
with unpredictable drops, changes in speed, and shifts in direction.

Sometimes you go on rollercoasters with people you know
and experience the highs and lows together.
Sometimes you ride with a stranger and, surprisingly,
you lean on one another when you are afraid,
or engage with one another during exhilarating moments.

Once you get off the rollercoaster, you are consumed with emotions.
Despite the twists and turns and frightening moments,
you enjoyed the thrill and quickly want to get back on the ride.
On the contrary, the ride could have been so scary you vow to never
get on this particular ride, nor a ride similar to it ever again.
The point is—you did it.

People can be bystanders and have an idea of what to expect,
but they truly do not know the rollercoaster until they have
experienced it themselves.
This is life.
The only way to truly know the thrill of life
is to experience it for yourself.

BLACK AND ARMED

No white fragility,
No white tears,
No micro-aggressions,
No white guilt,
No discrimination,
No racism
formed against you shall prosper.

Armor yourself with knowledge.
Know your rights.
Armor yourself with action.
Know how to, skillfully and systematically,
stand up for yourself and fight.
Armor yourself with faith.
Trust and believe that the enemy will not win.
Armor yourself with a deep sense of self-awareness.
The more you know who you are, they can't tell you who to be.

HURT PEOPLE WON'T HURT YOU

We often try to support and encourage
a loved one experiencing pain.
In return, they can, unintentionally or intentionally,
project and inflict their pain on you.
In the process of trying to fix
a loved one's broken pieces,
you can get cut.
Hurt people hurt people,
but you do not have to continuously stick around
to experience this hurt.

Being supportive, loving, encouraging, and "there"
is not measured by your ability to endure pain and toxicity.
As difficult as it may be,
you must remove yourself from this dynamic.
Remember, your wellbeing is always the priority.

YOU ARE THE LIMIT

They say the sky is the limit.
But, I disagree.
Saying the sky is the limit
to a woman who understands
her worth and value,
is too small.
You are beyond the beyond;
and far exceed the sky.

Sis, YOU are the limit because you are limitless.

THE GAME

The game is not set up in your favor.

My definition of "the game" is any area of life,
in which you are working to achieve
your personal definition of success—
career, business, romance, education, asset ownership, etc.

The game is barely set up for black women to play at all.
It, sure as hell, is not set up for us to win.
The established game rules are set in place for us to lose.
Does this mean if we play the game, we cannot win?
Hell no!

Play the game and see it through.
You can bet your ass you will lose 100% of the games you do not
play, including the ones you forfeit.
It doesn't matter if you come across challenges, have to reset,
and it takes you 10,000 tries,
never fold under pressure.

It's hard but it's not impossible—
You can win this game, sis.

COMMUNITY OF LOVE AND SUPPORT

We lean on our close community of love and support
when we are having bad days and
going through tough times.
You process encouragement based on the gravity of your situation,
how you feel,
and your coping mechanisms.

Sometimes the "everything will be okay" messages help.
Sometimes they can seem dismissive.
Sometimes the "stay strong, you got this" messages
remind you of your magic.
Sometimes they annoy you.
Sometimes the "push forward" messages
encourage you to keep going,
but sometimes thinking of the future hurts.

Tell your community of love how they can best support you.
This can change as you heal and process,
but continue to communicate your needs.

ACTIVATE YOUR LIGHT

It is easier to activate your light
when you are surrounded by light.
The hard part is learning how to shine in the darkness.
We all experience dark times.
Therefore, you must learn
how to activate your light
while the darkness surrounds you.

This can be done by having a
powerful connection to your light.
Consistently remind yourself
of your worth, brilliance, and purpose.
Train yourself to recognize your power and divine energy.
Frequently own that you are the universe.

Your light will guide you through the darkness
so that nothing can stand in your way.

FLOW LIKE LAVA

Lava is slow-moving, unstoppable, and strong.
Scientists have tried to figure this out,
but you cannot stop lava.

Have a flow like lava—
Slow and steady.
With strength that will demolish
any barriers that stand in its way,
and an unstoppable force.

FAKE IT UNTIL YOU MAKE IT

The "fake it until you make it" mindset is
faking confidence, comfort, love, optimism,
competence, interest, or happiness
until you make it a reality.

I recognize that "fake it until you make it"
can be a survival mindset.
But, it is not sustainable.
Eventually, this can get exhausting
and can take a toll on you.

It is unrealistic to suggest a complete erasure of
the "fake it until you make it," mindset
because black women are frequently in misogynistic,
racist, discriminatory, and
uncomfortable spaces that impact their livelihoods.

One may have to fake comfort
in a toxic work environment
around racism, misogyny, and xenophobia, to have peace.

Short term "fake it until you make it" survival tactics
can be coping mechanisms,
if you simultaneously work to address the problem,
or have plans in motion to get to
your authentic definition of "making it."

EMPLOYEE OF THE MONTH

It is YOUR job
to make sure you are happy, loved,
valued, and appreciated.
Do your job so well
you are employee of the month!

MIGHTY THOUGHTS

Your mind is the source of your power.
Everything you want for yourself starts in your mind,
with your thoughts.
Thoughts drive your decisions.
Thoughts can be agents of healing.
Thoughts have the ability to change your circumstances.
Water your thoughts with love.
Be kind to your thoughts.
Be patient with your thoughts.
Share your thoughts with those you trust.
Think.
Speak.
Do.
Deliver.

DEFINING SUCCESS

Be sure to personalize success and
know that your definition of it can change
as you grow and evolve.
Do not limit your definition of success
because of your fears.
Success can be related to career, business,
finances, profession, or possessions.
But remember, success also includes peace, joy,
love, growth, and understanding your value.
Do not allow anyone else to define success for you.
Do not allow anyone to make you feel
you should be content with anything
that is less than
the definition of success you are striving for.

PREPARE FOR WHAT YOU WANT

Expecting the best and
preparing for the worst
allows you to put energy into things
you do not truly want.
You do not want "the worst" to take away
from your best.

Expect the best.
Prepare for the best.
You will receive the best.

Expect the best.
Work for the best.
You will receive the best.

STRONG FRIEND

Hey, Strong Friend. I see you. I am you.
You are there for everyone else;
You are the go-to person for advice;
You wear your Strong Friend title with pride.

But, this title does not serve you.
Strong Friend, but you deal with your challenges alone.
Strong Friend, but you struggle in silence.
Strong Friend—you're a fixer for everyone while you feel broken.
Strong Friend, but you cannot be vulnerable
for the sake of everyone.
This is not helpful to you.

Your true friends do not want you to suffer in silence.
Your true friends do not want you to feel alone.
Your true friends will support you.
Articulate how you feel,
redefine your role as a friend, and
take care of yourself.

NEW NEW

People will say you're "acting funny" or
"acting brand new" when you, finally,
put yourself before them.

Oh, hello, Queen of Comedy.
What is that fragrance you're wearing?
New car smell?
Go New New!
If prioritizing you makes anyone feel anything
other than happy for your evolution,
there is no space for them in your life.

CHANGE FOR GROWTH

There are many areas in life where
you are bomb and kicking ass.
But, there are some areas that demand
change of thoughts, actions,
behaviors, and perspectives.

Do not drink that instant change Kool-Aid
because it will not work.

Change is not something that happens overnight—
be patient.
Commit to change,
but go at a comfortable pace
that is sustainable.

UNAPOLOGETICALLY, BLACK

Black culture is timeless and not just a trend.
Wear your hoops as big as you want.
Wear your natural hair to that interview.
Roll your neck and eyes when you are annoyed.
Tongue pop when you want to add emphasis to your words.
Wear your bundles and braids past your butt.
Put on lashes as long as you want them to be.
Keep snappin' and clackin' with your acrylic long nails.
Lay your hair and edges down and swoop your bang like never before.

Do not let anyone make you feel bad for being unapologetically, black.
Do you, sis!

BLACK AND PROUD

You can love Maroon 5 and be black and proud.
You can love anime and black and proud.
You can identify as emo, alt, or
be "Goth" and be black and proud.
You can love sci-fi and comic books
and be black and proud.
You can be into cosplay and be black and proud.
You can exclusively speak grammatically
and be black and proud.

Erasure of blackness because of
your musical preferences,
the way you speak, or your friends
is bullshit.

Do not let anyone define blackness for you
or minimize your blackness!

GRACE

Beautiful Black Queen,
you identify with the word grace,
as it relates to being poised,
but you do not give yourself grace,
as it relates to forgiving and being kind to you.

Give yourself permission to be human.
Give yourself permission to make mistakes.
Give yourself permission to learn and grow.
Please forgive you
in the way you are willing
to forgive and be kind to others.

YOUR NEXT CHAPTER

The next chapter of your book
is going to be the plot twist that
propels your entire book
into a bestselling novel.
Keep writing, sis!

HEALTHY COMPARISON

Comparison is toxic
when you are harmfully envious,
consistently focused on others,
and find yourself being a full-blown hater.
But comparison can be healthy
when you use it as inspiration.
Look at people in spaces you aspire to be
as they show you the possibilities.
Compare, take notes, collaborate,
and know that your season is on the horizon.

PAUSING THE EMOTIONAL REACTION

Queen,
You may find yourself in situations
where you want to react to someone or something
from unpleasant emotions that have taken over.

Give yourself time, space, and grace
to make the best moves for you!
This may take a lot of practice, but
the following steps will help you
navigate these situations.

1. *Reflect*
Think about the emotions you feel and the situation you are in. Is responding from the root of your current emotion drastically different from how you would handle this situation in a normal mindset?
Does it require an instant response or reaction or can you choose to react later?
Do you have something to lose if your reaction impacts the situation?
2. *Reset*
Pause. Take a break or sleep on it.
3. *Recheck*
Did you wake up feeling the same emotions regarding the situation?
Were there things you perhaps misunderstood?
Will you address the situation, or will it be best for you to let it go?
4. *React*
Choose a course of action that works best for you.

SELF-GRATITUDE

Oftentimes we practice gratitude
by being grateful for essentials—
money, food, and jobs.
This is necessary,
but you must also reflect on what you're grateful for
as it relates to who you are.
By doing this, you will increase your depth of self-awareness
because you often reflect on you.
Be grateful for your ability to be resilient.
Be grateful for your humor.
Be grateful for your kind heart.
Be grateful for self-confidence.
Be grateful for your creativity…
Keep it going!

GOD'S PLAN

Sometimes things don't go according to YOUR plan,
but they are going according to God's plan.
When God's plan is in motion, do not fight it.
Trust and go with it.
God's plan is far superior to yours.

PEACE

Queen, please prioritize peace in your life.
Oftentimes choosing peace means you have to let go of
relationships, jobs, behaviors, habits, and people.
This is not always easy, but it is necessary
because peace does not share space with toxicity,
disrespect, bullshit, or drama.

When you experience things in life that disturb your peace,
seek support to help
and discover tools to restore peace in your life.
When peace consumes your mind, body, and soul,
you understand its true value.
Hold it with high regard,
and you do everything in your power to hold on tight.

ALREADY A WINNER

You are not ENTERING your winning season,
you're already a winner.
Change your mindset, Queen!

SELF-AWARENESS

Self-awareness is the key to your universe.
You must know who you are,
what brings out different emotions,
what your boundaries are,
what helps you to recharge, and
how you give and receive love,
to understand how you can use your magic,
wield the universe to your demands,
and activate all your power.

CHASING NEXT

Black women are the most educated.
Black women are driven.
Black women are shattering glass ceilings.
Black women are still making history as
"the first black woman", in every field.
Chasing "next" is what you do because you are driven
and will not settle.
With every barrier you break,
every milestone you reach,
every dream that comes true for you,
you must celebrate!
You must smell the roses!
Enjoy the view and the fruits of your labor!
You can keep your eyes on the prize.
But take in the glory!
Take in the victories!
Do not allow chasing next to diminish
the value of your "now."

HONESTY BEFORE MANIFESTING

Before you begin manifesting things
you want in your life,
you must be honest with yourself.
What are your heart and soul's true needs and desires?
Confirm and then manifest them!
Do not manifest things you truly do not believe in
or do not want.
If you do, you will be using your divine energy
to breathe life into things that do not feed your soul.
Set your intentions and be clear about what you want.
Demand it, work for it,
believe in it, and you will receive it!

PERCEPTIONS

Perceptions are not reality,
they are subjective.
Do not alter who you are to coddle
assumed or confirmed perceptions.
If they want to see you as their definition of the
"angry black woman," they will.
If they want to see you as their definition of
"ghetto," they will.
Do not work hard to control the narrative
when you're not the author of the story.
Be you.
Do you.
Middle finger to them.

BET ON YOU

Go all in on you.
The best bet, I can guarantee you will win
is betting on you.
I know that is easier said than done,
for a lot of us.
I know you must do self-work
before you go all in and bet on you.
But once you get there, hold on,
continue to stay with your bet,
have faith, and you will win 10 times as much
as you initially put in.
This will be the best reward.

BE PROUD OF YOU

Pride is the feeling of gratification for one's accomplishments.
To be satisfied with your accomplishments
you must acknowledge the hard work, discipline,
and dedication it took for you to see your goal come to fruition.
Black women are extremely driven and
sometimes we do not pause
to experience satisfaction for our achievements.

How often do you experience pride?
Reflect on the frequency in which you have felt most proud
and compare it to the things you deem to be accomplishments.
Are you truly giving yourself enough credit
for all you have accomplished?
Sometimes we have a perfectionist mentality.
We refuse to accept our accomplishment as deserving of pride,
unless it has achieved some level of perfection.
We must remember to celebrate and acknowledge all of our
achievements, big or small.

Having pride in our accomplishments reinforces our purpose
and allows us to show self-appreciation for our dedication.
Celebrating accomplishments boosts self-esteem
and motivates us to take the necessary step towards
achieving the next goal.

REDEFINING COMFORT ZONE

If you talk about needing to get out of your comfort zone,
there is nothing comfortable in it.
Referring to this as a comfort zone
minimizes the discomfort you feel in this space.
Whether you are itching to try new things,
challenge yourself, or chase your dreams,
this space is restricting and does not welcome growth.
Once you acknowledge that you are not in a comfort zone,
work on a plan to take steps towards something even greater—
a freedom zone.

PERFECT WORLD CHALLENGE

Write out your perfect world.
Think of no limits.
No racism and discrimination
that can stand in your way.
No misogyny that can stand in your way.
No financial issues that can stand in your way.
No physical or mental challenges
that can stand in your way,
No YOU standing in your way.

What does your life look?
What are you doing for your career or business?
How are you loved, give love,
and show love to yourself?
Where are you located?
What do your vacations look like?

Write out every single thing you would have
in your perfect world. You can add to this every day.
This exercise allows you to see your soul's true desires
without limits or restrictions.
There are several things you will write in this perfect world
that may seem impractical.
Understand you are the limit, which means
you are limitless,
you can have this perfect world.

YOU ARE NOT OKAY

It is okay to not be okay.
Actually, it is more than okay to not be okay.
It is expected for you to not always be okay.
Think of all the times we have had to keep going, as a people,
and adopt a mindset that we must be okay,
despite our many obstacles.

We have to survive murder, unexplainable violence,
systematic oppression, family separation, and so much trauma.
Look at what we have built while facing these monstrous
challenges.

We have had to go in survival mode by normalizing pain
as a part of life and strongly believing we are okay,
when we are not.
If we say we are okay, maybe we will be okay.
It saddens me that we have to normalize not being okay.
Give yourself permission to tell you and your circle of love—
I am not okay.
Then move on to what that means to you,
process, and focus on healing.

SISTER SHORTCUTS

You do not have to take the scenic route
to get to where you want to go.
Take advice, follow blueprints,
find a mentor, trust your gut,
go with your divine energy,
and follow energies that align with yours.
Remember, our ancestors crawled so we can fly!
There is a sister that worked her ass off to build a bridge,
so you can make it to the other side easier than she did.

BYOB

Be your own boss.
Take ownership of your life—
stand firm in who you are.
Create a lane for yourself.
Bring your authentic self in whatever space you are in.
You are a B.O.S.S.
Brilliant
Outstanding
Strong, and
Successful.

BULLETS FIRED AT BULLETPROOF ARMOR

Assertive. Aggressive. Angry.
These are words used as weapons
against black women.
Please do not allow these words to disturb your peace.
Let them call you assertive.
Assertive means you are confident and
can articulate what you want and need.
You are an advocate for yourself
because in many situations,
no one else is going to advocate for you.

Let them call you aggressive.
Aggressive means you do not back down, and
you face confrontation head on.
In many situations, we must be aggressive,
as we face the most disrespect in the world.

Let them call you angry.
We have every reason to be angry.
We are mistreated, abused, disrespected,
devalued and gaslit while we are expected to give,
nurture, succeed, and support.
This is unfair.
They want to use these words as weapons,
but they will not penetrate your soul
because you are black and armored.

OWNERSHIP OF GREATNESS

You may have had guidance and help along the way,
but you are experiencing greatness because of you.
You are thriving because you put in the work.
You are smiling because you have found the keys to unlock joy.
You are responsible for your own success, healing, and happiness.
No one else can take credit for who you are.
You can have gratitude for those who have helped you,
but be sure to take ownership of your greatness.

EXPECTATIONS

Expectations allow you to create standards for yourself,
your relationships, career, education, and
the spaces you navigate.
You are the best, the baddest,
and setting the expectations for reciprocity is a MUST.

If you believe and trust that you are dope,
why should you not expect dopeness in return?

Expect to receive with the same force you give.

CAREFREE LIGHT

One of the most amazing things to see
is a black woman being her beautiful, carefree self.
A black Queen that walks in the room and owns it.
A black Queen on the dance floor with all eyes on her.
A black Queen that can challenge bullshit
with facts and knowledge.
A black Queen that defies all social norms and
does not aim to please anyone but her damn self.
A black Queen that goes against the grain
and does things her way.

They will try to make her the villain because
she is the victor and does not conform.
Living in a carefree light blazes a trail of confidence and pure joy.
She will rise and inspire other black women
to activate their carefree light
so, her victories multiply.

DUE PRIVILEGES

You are entitled to (your definition of) success.
You are entitled to happiness.
You are entitled to love.
You are entitled to self-forgiveness.
You are entitled to self-care.
You are entitled to protection.
You are entitled to respect.
You are entitled to make mistakes.
Remove any barriers that exist to block these things for you.

YOU GOT IT

You either have it or
you ~~don't~~ have not accessed it.

You GOT IT and if no one else has told you,
I am telling you.
Maybe you did not have it when
you thought you should?
That was not meant for you.
Please do not give up until you find it.

CHANGING FACES

Mindsets you were taught and socialized to adopt
may not align with your beliefs and values today.
Allow yourself space to sort through these internal conflicts.

The internal conflict may arise because
announcing your new beliefs could alter family dynamics,
your romantic relationship, friendships, or your work life.
This can be very difficult to navigate.

But, do not allow anyone to take you away from
being and loving your best self,
freely expressing yourself, and
having optimal wellness.
Live your life for you and
distance or remove yourself from
anyone that prevents this.

REDEFINING SELF-CARE

The images of self-care typically include massages at the spa—
Bath robes, face masks, and mani/pedis.
Trips around the world.
Meditation and yoga.
Luxury.
These are amazing ways to take care of yourself,
but this isn't sustainable for daily self-care.
Self-care is anything you do to consciously take care
of your mind, body, and soul.
Self-care is what you make of it.
It is important for you to take care of you.
Redefine self-care and what it means for you.

MAGNITUDE OF YOUR MAGIC

Discover the magnitude of your magic, sis!
People will try to hex, curse, and put spells on you.
But when you know you are a powerful sorceress,
you know they do not stand a chance.
You know there is magic flowing from
every inch of your being.
You don't even waste your time
convincing them of your power.
You exude confidence because
you know who you are.
Let them try you, you bad-ass mighty sorceress!

TRUTHS TOLD BY THE BODY

Your body speaks truths
that you deny your soul.
When you put the weight of the world
on your shoulders and
cannot find the words to understand why
you are out of alignment—listen to your body.
Be honest with yourself
to discover the mental root of
your physical discomfort.

NO TRAP QUEENS

You are not stuck.
You always have options.
They may not be convenient.
They may not be comfortable.
But when you feel stuck and trapped,
convenience and comfort will eventually
be on the other side
once you make it through.
Making it through may seem so impossible, but
it will happen if you do the work (whatever that looks like to you)
and move in a healthy way.

TOXIC ENERGY

You know where all the external toxic energy
comes from in your life.
You are in love with them.
You have been friends with them since
back in the day.
You see potential in your relationship with them.
You cannot tap into your divine energy when
you are surrounded by toxicity.
It is not easy to get out of toxic environments
when you are deeply invested.
But seeds of prosperity, abundance, and
growth cannot be planted in toxicity.
Prioritize what truly matters most...you!

FINGERPRINT UNIQUE

Be as unique and individualized
as your fingerprint.
Some people will discourage you or
try to convince you to conform to group thinking
when you are your true you.
Some people will celebrate and love you
and be inspired by your true you.
Ultimately, you want to be in a position where you do not need
others to validate being your true you.
Whatever you do, do it as authentically YOU as possible.

RECEIVING LOVE

Allow yourself to be loved and cared for
in the way you love and care for others.

KNOW TO GROW

Knowledge is power.
Put yourself in spaces where you can
learn and evolve.
Read books.
Listen to audiobooks.
Listen to podcasts.
Learning is important to our evolution and growth.
In the words of my Uncle Buck,
"you must know to grow!"
When you expand your knowledge,
you expand your capacity for growth.

OVERFLOW

Excessively pour into your cup, so
you do not give from your cup,
you give from the overflow.

YOU ARE A WHEN-NER

Be specific about what you want and
choose language that breathes life into
all that you desire.
Start by speaking on your desires
in a way that illustrates your confidence that
they will come to life.
Remove "if" and only speak about "when."

When you get your dream job...
When you accomplish all of your goals...
When you find the love of your life...
When you heal and make it through difficulties...
When you deeply love and trust yourself...

Use language that reflects what you are:
mighty, magical, and powerful.

A FORCE WHEN YOU KNOW IT

You are a movement by yourself.
But you are an unstoppable force when you remember
that you are a movement.
Constantly remind yourself of your force.

DO NOT QUIT

You are on the brink of all
you have been working so hard for.
All of your hard work will not be in vain.
All the bullshit you have dealt with
will not be in vain.
Whatever you do, do not quit.

NEW DAY, WHO DIS?

Today is a new day and
you will not be shaken or discouraged.
Today is a new day and
you will not let the remnants of yesterday's negativity
destroy the positive energy you want to create on this day.
Today is a new day and
you will not forget to activate your goddess light.
Use the energy of the new day to reset,
restore, and move forward.

YOU

Choose you.
Save yourself first.
You are the priority.
You are the prize.
You are the one.
Chase you.
It is always you.

KARMA

Staying in an unhealthy situation
for the sake of avoiding "bad karma"
is unfair to you.
Choosing you and removing yourself will
sometimes inconvenience (not hurt or harm)
others in the process, that is okay.
Know that the good karma you were deserving of before leaving
will still come to you.

LIFE DANCE

No one else knows the choreography
to the life dance routine, you create.
Oftentimes, you will have flawless performances
and the audience will throw flowers on stage as
a sign of appreciation and love.
What happens when you mess up a routine?
Keep going!
Go with the flow and allow your intuition to lead the way.
You will still receive those flowers for a job well done.
While the mess up will seem devastating and drastic to you,
no one noticed because you carried on with the routine.

HEALING WOUNDS

Time heals wounds.
Time alone does not.
You must take care of the wound—
properly clean and examine it, and over time,
the wound will heal.
Soul and emotional wounds can cut so deep
you cannot quite understand how
you are going to move on in life with this pain.
You don't know HOW to take care of the wound.
You can't properly care for the wound alone and
you feel you have no one to help.
If there is someone in your life you trust,
please tell them you need help
taking care of this wound.
If you feel alone and you do not have anyone to go to,
look for communities where you can find people
dealing with your specific wound.
With love, care, help, and time, your wounds will heal.

TIME

Time is precious.
Time is fragile.
Time is not guaranteed.
Time is taken for granted.
If you're reading this, the time is now.
Research how to start your business and do it.
Call that friend you have been thinking about.
Write that book.
Go to therapy and work on healing.
Whatever is burning in your soul to be released—
Do it.

BUBBLE OF NOTHING

Remember when I said you are the universe?
I told no lies.
But sis, it is exhausting to BE the universe and
control/oversee everything in it.
Allow yourself to have moments and days where you create
a bubble of stillness.
Pause the hustle,
remove yourself from those kids,
tell bae to give you some space,
step away from the traumatic news, and
find your calm.
You may be saying "girl bye, I do not have time for this bubble you
speak of."
Trust me, I get it.
Start with a 5-minute bubble and
expand it when you can.
Moments of calm, stillness,
pause, and nothingness are necessary
to hold your universe together.

BYE DOUBT

When doubt tries to infiltrate your mind,
tell doubt "step aside, I got this."
And, be specific about what you got!
Own your greatness by acknowledging what you are great at.
Tell your doubts you know what you're doing and
give them examples.
Doubt is no match for confidence!

INVESTING IN YOU

Invest in people that add positivity to your life.
Once you can identify the negative people and negative energy,
distance or remove yourself.
Invest in making peace with your past.
Talk things out with your community of love and support,
go to a coach or therapist,
find resources to help you build the tools to confront things that
haunt you, and
know that peace with your past will allow you to heal in the
present.

Invest in your standards.
Work to create a deep understanding of your definitions of
respect, boundaries, and expectations.
Identify internal and external behaviors that violate your
standards. This will help to uphold your standards.

Invest in yourself.
Go full force on taking care of you.
Evaluate areas in your life where you can give more to you.
Investing in self will be the greatest investment you ever make.

PRICE OF PEACE

No one in this universe can afford your peace;
it is top tier currency—priceless.

POSSESSION OF POWER

You possess the power within to turn your dreams into reality.
You possess the power within to change your life.
You possess the power, magic, and wisdom from your ancestors.
All that you need to reach your greatest potential is within you.

BIG DREAMS>SMALL MINDS

When you have big dreams,
people around you may try to project
their insecurities and doubts onto you…
DO NOT allow them to!
Your dreams may seem impossible to small minds.
They'll tell you "no one else has done this" or
"maybe you should play it safe."
DO NOT listen to them!
Black women are trailblazers.
At some point in time,
the "play it safe" mentality these small minds want for you, today,
was the "impossible" for black women of the past.
Surround yourself with encouraging and supportive people.
Big dreams overpower small minds.

GO HARDER!

Getting what you want out of life is determined by your effort.
If you want more and you're in a space to go harder,
do it, sis.
Excellence is created by excellent effort.
Make shit happen!

PROTECT WHAT YOU PROJECT

Beautiful Black Queen,
you are the universe composed of all things.
Not everyone deserves to have access to your magic,
make them earn it!
If you project love, you protect it
by giving access to people worthy of your love.
If you project kindness, you protect your kind spirit
by giving access to people deserving of your kindness.
Protect what you want to project.

SAY NO

Floetry says, "all you gotta do is say yes."
I say to you: you have to say "no,"
Not right now,
I cannot,
I do not have the time,
I am unavailable,
I decline (not regretfully or apologetically).

Too many times you say "yes" at your own expense, Queen.
You are not wrong for saying "no."
Let them call you selfish and mean.
Eventually, the feelings that have you
apprehensive to say "no"
will go away.

LET GO AND HOLD ON

Let IT go.
Let THEM go.
Hold on to YOU!

TRANSFORMATIVE GROWTH

You are not being dramatic when you articulate your emotions.
Middle finger to anyone who dare calls you a
drama queen for doing so.
You may have minimized past experiences as a coping mechanism,
but now you are identifying challenges and actively working to heal.
Each day you make it,
please remember that you worked hard to make it through that day.
The sucky days truly suck,
but do not allow them to diminish your progress.
You are giving it your all,
your transformation is inspiring,
and no one can take away your personal growth.

COLOR AND LIGHTING

A color can look different based on the lighting.
A color can appear to be a dull tone in dark lighting.
Then, vibrant and bright in natural lighting.
It can glow in the dark under black lights.
You have the right color, sis!
Just change your lighting to fit your preference.

MOVE FORWARD

Advice, feedback, support, and guidance are wonderful.
But make sure you are not at a standstill because you are waiting
on others to give you permission to move forward.
No one is going to be invested in you the way you are.
Trust in your abilities and start your journey.

GO TO THE FACTS

Lead with your worth.
Let your worth guide your work.
Your environment should reflect your worth.
Your worth will align with your work.
If you cannot see your worth,
turn to the facts…

Write down all you do in your workplace.
Write down what you do as a friend.
Write down who you are as partner.
Write down what you do for family.
Then assess how you are being treated.
Are you being valued and appreciated?

BELIEVE IN YOU

You will never lose if you truly believe you can win!

TRAGEDY IS TRAGEDY

You do not have to turn tragedy into triumph.
You do not have to turn your sorrows into motivation.
You do not have to hurry up and bounce back.
Tragedy is sometimes just tragedy and
doesn't have to immediately be the prerequisite or
catalyst to triumph.
You owe it to yourself to heal, to feel,
to process, to breathe.

MOVE LOUD AND PROUD

Move in silence with everyone that is not in your inner circle,
but move loud and proud with your community of love and support!
Whatever journey you are embarking on will be very difficult,
especially if you try to do it alone.
Ask for support as you navigate change.
Share your developed thoughts and ideas during the infancy stages.
Seek honest feedback and be open to constructive criticism.
If you do not have a community of love and support, find online
groups related to what you are doing and use them as a resource.
No matter what, please do not completely do this alone.

THANK YOU ANCESTORS

So many times, we hear about the trauma we have inherited
from our ancestors.
While this may be true,
let's not forget we also inherited their strength,
grace, passion, and power.
The spirit of your ancestors lives within you,
they surround you, and they guide you.
We are the universe they created.
Embrace them.
Honor them.
And never forget—
you are the manifestation of their hopes and dreams.

SKILLS AND WILL

If you have the skills and will to go after your dreams, do it.
With a power combination of abilities and attitude,
you will be just fine!
If you don't have the EXACT skills you need,
for your dreams, do not give up.
Re-evaluate and see how you can couple
your strengths and skills with your passion.
If what you are looking for does not exist,
build it yourself!

CONGRATULATIONS!

Congratulations, you have broken generational curses!
Congratulations, you have tapped into your magic and
understand you ARE the universe!
Congratulations, you will not take shit from not even YOU when try
to stand in your own way!
Congratulations, you are standing in your truth and
owning who you are!
Congratulations, you don't give a damn about
what they say or think about you!
Congratulations, your bank account is showing numbers
you have never seen before!
Congratulations, you not only love your whole being, but you have
also found love from the partner of your dreams!
Congratulations on all that you have and will accomplish, sis!

SLOW PROGRESS

Slow progress can be the same as no progress if you have
the ability to speed up progress.
Why would progress go slow if you have the time,
resources, and ability to speed it up?
Sometimes slow progress is a reflection of your disconnection
to where you are heading.
Take a step back and reflect on your true desires.
You may find that you no longer want
to make progress in that direction.

YOU ARE WORTHY

Daily reminder:

You are the universe.

You are more than enough.

You are worthy of all thing glorious.

You are worthy of more than what you give yourself.

Your worth will guide your work, wellness, and wealth.

HIDDEN GEMS WITHIN

You have only scratched the surface of who you are destined to be.
There are gems you have buried so deep in the depths of you
that you do not have access to.
Sometimes your gems are hidden because you were discouraged
and told they were not beautiful,
you tried to access them before you were ready
and things did not go well, or you do not know they exist.

If you do the "Perfect World" challenge (p. 45),
you may notice many hidden gems.
When you discover these hidden gems,
learn about all the characteristics that make them beautiful and
how they fit into your life.
When you are ready, shine bright and show them off, beautiful!

REJECTION

Rejection hurts.
Rejection makes you question your abilities.
Rejection can crush your confidence.
People will tell you to quickly move on from rejection,
but I encourage you to feel your feels and
process when you are ready.
Once you recover, you realize rejection protects you
from things that are not meant for you.
Rejection is not truly the textbook definition of rejection.
Rejection can propel you to the next level.
Rejection can motivate and inspire you.
Rejection can be the pivot that gets you going in the right
direction.
Everything that is for you will come to you.
Everything that is for you will work out for you.

LIVE

Working to create mental, physical, emotional,
educational, and financial optimal wellness is exhausting.
Do not forget about this beautiful life of yours.
Please do me a favor and do the following:

Laugh out loud—like that good old "auntie" laugh!
Dance. Turn on your favorite songs and vibe out.
Smile that external-display-of-your-internal-peace-and-joy smile.
Put your best outfit together and show out.
Wear what makes you feel good.
Wear your comfy clothes and binge watch your favorite show.
Stand in the sun and admire your glow.
Cross off things on your bucket list.
Make beautiful memories with the people you love.
Make beautiful memories with strangers.
Allow the thrill of adventure to outweigh fear.
Send that text message that you may regret in the morning.
Create—in whatever way you have been gifted with creativity.

Sis, please live!

PART 2: WORDS OF LOVE AND ADVICE TO BLACK WOMEN FROM BLACK WOMEN

Love yourself and know your worth. No one will love you as deeply as you can love yourself. You cannot depend on anyone else to give you the love your heart desires. It has to be within you. Know that you are beautiful and forget anyone that tries to make you think of yourself in any other way!

Everyone will not treat you like you treat them. When you recognize this, you give what they give. If this is an unhealthy relationship, you have to move on. I know it's hard to turn your love off and on, but you will get tired of being sick and tired and you will do it; everyone has a breaking point.

If there's something you want to accomplish, don't let anyone stop you from doing so. While you're in the process of working towards your goals, people will throw their negativity on you. They are envious because you're doing something that they wish they had the courage to do. People will tell you what you shouldn't do but when you do it and you're successful (because you will be), then they want to be on your team and roll with you; be sure to tell them HELL NO!

When you have your mind made up, you do what's best for you. If you still can't make up your mind, get your heart right, listen to it, and come up with something for yourself. Through good times and bad, know that you got this and you will be just fine!

Phyllis French
(My beautiful mother)

Be the bright, brilliant, and beautiful person that you are and don't let anyone or anything steer you away from your dreams. Go above and beyond your own expectations to reach your goals and dreams. Spell out what success means for you because it is different for each person. There is no easy route to success. Sadly, some people will try to encourage you to skip steps in the ladder to success because they want to see you fall. Walk away from those people that don't mean you well. Work hard, remain focused and determined, and do not be afraid of failure. The only time you truly fail is when you stop trying.

In life, you will have highs and lows, challenges, tests, and testimonies. Put your big girl panties on and knock out each obstacle that comes your way. Every challenge that you face is an opportunity to grow and improve. Look in the mirror, smile, give yourself a hug, love yourself, believe in yourself, and celebrate you every day.

Nikki Green
Facebook: K.Nicole Creations
Instagram: @k.nicolecreations
(My beautiful sister)

It's okay to start from square one as long as you don't allow that to be the only square you focus on in life. Sometimes we have to go back to the beginning of our own stories to reflect, heal, and unlearn unhealthy behaviors we didn't realize we had. You should not punish yourself as you work to improve and get rid of these behaviors. You have to forgive the YOU of the past that you are working to heal. Speak positivity into yourself when you are on this journey.

As you heal, grow, improve, and move on from square one, you may look at the people you surround yourself with in a different light. If you notice that you're in a constant race with people in your inner circle, trample over them bitches and move on. You may have to run by yourself for a while, but you will meet others that give you the same help, support, positivity, and sisterhood you give to everyone else. I wish nothing but love, growth, and winning for you!

Whitney French
Instagram: @_livin4me
(My beautiful sister)

Sistah, Queen, Black Wombman!

You are a light, brightly shining. Star.
You are the backbone of Nations. Strength.
You are adaptable like water.
Gentle like a cool mist on a hot day,
yet powerful like a Hurricane. Fluid.

You are the epitome of resilience. Unrelenting.
You are ever evolving. Transcending.

Sistah, Queen, Black Wombman!

Lift your head! The crown gets heavy, yes, it's true.
When it does your sistahs will surround you.
Your sistahs are within you. Your sistahs will lift you.
We are you. You are we.
We are she. She is you. Sistah.

Never settle Queen. Know your worth and
add a shipping and processing fee.
You are worth your weight in gold, just by being you.
Collect your taxes, Queen.

Black Wombman. Oooooooooh black Wombman!
It's your hair and the way it defies norms.
It's your melanin glowing in the sun.
It's the curve of your lips.
It's the sway of your body to the beat!
It's the melody of your voice.
It's your very presence that scares them.

Exist anyway! Be you anyway, Black wombman.
The sun doesn't dim her light for others.
Others must adapt to the sun.
You are the sun. You are the stars.

You are light. Brightly shining. You are strength.
You are the backbone of Nations.
You are adaptable like water.
You are ever evolving.
Transcending.

Sistah, Queen, Black Wombman.

Tamara Moody-Orise

Facebook: Galveston County's Black Owned Everything

Love is a beautiful thing! It is infectious, it is kind,
and it is the greatest healing energy....

I believe in love and romanticizing your life. You should cultivate
a relationship with yourself that is full of love, understanding,
compassion, and support.

Listen to yourself, embrace your intuition, learn your love
language, and focus on being in tuned with your wants, needs, and
boundaries.

Challenge yourself. Allow yourself time to self-reflect; especially
when you are confused or unsure.

Date yourself, get to know you! Grasp that inner peace.
You should continuously move in love. Be kind to yourself and
others.

Forgiveness is the ultimate expression of love. You must forgive;
forgive yourself, forgive those that have hurt you—forgive them
even if they don't ask for forgiveness (doesn't mean you have to
forget that lesson or let them back into your light). This forgiveness
is for you, your energy, and your light!

When we work on things that are for us, we truly develop self-
worth, confidence, and self-love.

The loving healthy relationship that you develop within yourself will
allow you to be your true authentic self wherever you go. BElieve in
YOUrself!

Shaton Harris

In life, the bad chapters are what makes the other chapters towards greatness feel better!

Find anything that inspires, encourages, and motivates you.

There's beauty in the struggle. It allows you to see how beautiful simple things are in life, such as the beauty of the sunrise or sunset.

Ciarra Moore
Author of *Life As We Grow and Flesh vs. Spirit: An Intellectual Battle*

*

You are so deeply missed Queen Ciarra. Thank you for being a part of my community of love and support. I know you have been with me as I have written this book for our sisters, beautiful angel in heaven.

Love always,
Your travel partner in spirit
Phylicia (Fe)

Practice feeling negative emotions.
It is difficult, but you will hurt yourself more by
pushing them aside and burying them.

Being vulnerable is not easy but tell yourself it is okay to feel bad.
It's okay to hurt—even though you do not want to.
You must recognize that you're hurt, and healing and
you will get better with time, but you have to really try.

Andrea Woods

What you get out of life is what you put into it, mentally.
Listen to your conscious if you have an unsure or icky feeling—
it's telling you that you are settling for less than what you deserve.
Last but not least, no outside entity will fulfill you.
Stop waiting for someone else to love you
because you don't want to love yourself.

Riham Mohammad
A Girl like You
Instagram: @riizi_27

Healing, Self-Love, and Peace: Recipes to Happiness

The first step of happiness for me was healing, the second step was self-love, and the third was protecting my peace. Once you master all, you become UNSTOPPABLE and you'll discover super powers you didn't know you had.

HEALING

I had to let go of childhood trauma and different situations that haunted me for decades. I'm not a confrontational person, so I held a lot in, which wasn't good because the "should have, could have, would haves" played in my head nonstop. Most of the time I hid my pain well with smiles, laughter, and good times. Some days I would just shut down from the whole world so I wouldn't spaz out. I used to get so angry, and I felt like I was MISUNDERSTOOD from a child to adulthood. You let people get away with so much, but then when you speak your mind "you're crazy." Bottling up all my emotions, feelings, and horrible memories took a toll on me and my health. The more I held things in, the more unhappy I was. I thought writing my emotions and problems down then burning them up would help. I thought talking to God would make everything better, but he wanted me to do more. In 2019, I started HEALING. I addressed people, situations, and broken relationships that bothered me for years. Although some secrets hurt me and others to the core, a huge weight was lifted off my shoulders. I felt like I had my life back. I felt like I had a voice. I felt free. I didn't want to go into 2020 with those burdens. With Covid-19 hitting us unexpectedly, quarantine gave me time to self-isolate and work on me, inside and out.

SELF LOVE

One day I looked in the mirror and told myself "I love you" and meant it.
Dear Queen, accept the person you are flaws and all.
Love yourself unconditionally.
Nobody's perfect!
Be you!
Know that your strength comes from the Lord.
Know that you are beautiful.
Know your worth.
Know that you are strong.
Know that you are in control of your own life and happiness.
Know that no one owes you anything but yourself.
Take time for yourself.
Spoil yourself.
Treat yourself how you want to be treated.
Change the things you can and don't stress about what you can't.

PROTECT YOUR PEACE

Protect your Peace by all means.
Meditate!
Find a hobby.
Visit your happy place.
Do things that make you happy.
Live for you.
Don't get caught up in negativity.
Uplift one another and be humble.
You never know what a person is going through
and you never know how life can change for you in a blink of an eye.
I'm still working on me, but I'm not where I used to be physically,

mentally, and emotionally. I'm growing and glowing every day. I hope sharing a little bit of me will help someone out there. Stop hiding behind the mask and walk in your truth with your head held high, QUEEN!

Key'erria Hill
Email: Keyerriahill@yahoo.com
Instagram: @key_errias_kreations

No matter the battle, keep on fighting and going until you reach the prize.
God gives his biggest battles to his strongest soldiers.
Big or small, God has already mapped out the victory.

Jasmine Bryant
Instagram: @ ___jasminenichole___

Hard Shit

Chin up, chest out
This li'l storm can't take me out
I may bend but I won't break
Giving up now would be a huge mistake
I can do this, one step at a time
There is no mountain too tall for me to climb
I am a strong woman, full of grit
I am a tough woman and I do hard shit

Trevor Simon

I Am Not

I am not my trauma
I am my triumph

I am not my sin
I am a walking blessing

I am not bound by victimhood
Because I will always be victorious

I am not who people say I am
I am who God created me to be

Stevonne Fuller
The Antithesis of Superwoman Podcast
Instagram: @antithesis_of_superwoman

Remember, everyone doesn't carry the same GRACE or ANOINT-ING as you. They may have the gift but it's the ANOINTING that activates it.

DO NOT allow others to compare you with people who don't carry what you carry!

You were born for this!
Walk in confidence and boldness of that which you were created for.
Guess what?
NOBODY can do it like YOU do!
- Edidiong "E.CHRYS" Obot

Instagram & Twitter: @e_chrys
LinkedIn: Edidiong Obot
Facebook: E.chrysobot
Clubhouse: @echrys
Let's collaborate: Campsite.bio/echrys

I exude brilliance even on my darkest days.
My soul is Majestic.
It blazes, passionately,
attracting my deepest desires in every way.

Ashley Taylor
Instagram: @_themajesticsoul
Facebook: TheMajesticSoul

Knowing your true self is knowing your life's purpose.
What is built in you is the foundation of your true purpose.
The more you wander on this earth, the more your spirit will yearn
to know its truth.
Finding your purpose is not easy when you do not know your true
identity, but the search is worth it.

God will have hidden treasures for you if you seek them,
through the power of prayer. We all go through stages in life where
we question why we are here and what God wants for us.
The answer is...God wants you!

When he gets your full attention, he can give you what you need to
truly see yourself.
He wants to clothe you with his honor and glory,
but you have to be willing to allow him to be a part of the search for
your purpose.

Your purpose is in your thoughts, future, and prayers.
Allow God to manifest the desires in your heart so you may be free
to understand your true purpose.
When you find the time to yield to Him,
he will take care of the rest because you are his child.

Crystal Vonshaè
Instagram: @crystal_vonshae_
Email: crystalvonshae@gmail.com

The beauty of a black woman runs skin deep.
The possession of her soul is her strength.
A masterpiece of divine power is her worth.
Consider your value and level up!

Valencia Puente

Words of encouragement always start from within.
I always say, "I wish I would have pushed myself a little harder for the goals I set."

Never doubt yourself; there is never a limit to your success or dreams as long as you know deep down you are working hard for you.

Never regret a mistake that was made in the past.
I always say it's just something that gave me a better push for the future. Looking back, there are three words I can use that put me where I am today: faith, determination and fearlessness.
Be free and follow the path in front of you.

Taylor Jacob
Instagram: @markeiajay

As human beings it is our natural inclination to want to avoid discomfort. However, discomfort is a part of the human condition and it is important to build tools to manage, minimize, or even sit with discomfort.

We often find ourselves procrastinating, avoiding or even ruminating on our discomfort. Subsequently, the discomfort takes control and is prolonged.

Alternatively, be proactive in managing your discomfort. Problem-solve, seek support, have the difficult conversations, choose your needs, and remember YOU are human.

Jennifer Wiggins MA, LPC
Email: jenniferwigginslpc@gmail.com

Love the person that's looking at you in the mirror.
You're all that you need to be!

Creshonda Collins
Facebook: Creshonda Collins

Surround yourself with positive like-minded people who will encourage you and support you on your journey towards greatness. I encourage you, today, to please let go of who you were in the past and embrace the new you. The past version of you no longer exists.

Fear is your biggest enemy. From fear comes doubts and from doubts you freeze and can't move forward.

Always be confident in yourself. Write down your thoughts, your future achievements, and your goals as a constant reminder of where you want to go, in case you forget sometimes.

Be direct and honest in how you show up in the world.
Have patience.
Prioritize self-care in your personal and professional life.
Don't let relationships fall to the wayside just because you're busy.
Find the time and make the time for those close to you and prioritize your well-being.

XO,

J. Spears
Instagram: @Iamjae30
Email: msjae40@gmail.com

I Am Woman. I Am Black.

I am woman
I am black

I am threatening to those who lack

For some reason it is believed
that I don't feel pain
So I often suffer silently
and fight to maintain

In childhood, womanhood,
childbirth, motherhood
In relationships, marriage,
in corporate America

In every domain,
it's the same
I'm expected to check my attitude
and stay in my lane

Don't speak too loud
Don't speak too proud

Don't speak too often
Approach with caution

Doing all of this,
hoping my image would soften
And beauty...

According to him,
you, and them—
My attractiveness is slim

It's reiterated in real life,
music, and film
Leaving self-esteem grim
From childhood,
black girls are sexualized
We're told, "oh no,
you can't wear those shorts,
they show your thighs."

We face ludicrous accusations
Even when we are the powerless ones
in the situation

We become victims to
those of our own relation
Our own blood,
our own kin
And adults yell "who you think you are,
trying to temp grown men?"

In my head,
I'm thinking,
"how am I tempting a grown man?
 I'm only 10."
But see,
I figured out
what this act is—

It's deeply rooted
in anti-blackness

It's rooted in self-hate
And you want to force feed me
and keep refilling my plate
I am no longer staying
in the prison that you create

I see my beauty, I see my strength
And with my strength,
I see my femininity

And I won't allow you to tell me
my features resemble masculinity

You see,
I can go at this in length
Because frankly,
I am tired of your shit

Simply because,
I am woman
I am black

I am threatening
because you lack
I have my power
under lock and key
and you can't have it back

And not only that—

The power,
this power, I keep
I'm going to share it with
EVERY black girl,
black woman I meet

Torri Reed
Instagram: @torri.reed

Love

Until I learned to love myself, I couldn't love another soul!

New Beginnings

Yesterday's problems were yesterday's problems, today is a new day!

Geneva Cano

Through It All

This is coming from someone who was raised in the trenches.
I'm from an island where opportunities were small to none.
My mother struggled with seven kids,
so my sister and I were raised by my grandmother.
This is just a small glance at my story.

I take all the negativity and turn it into positivity.
Why?
I've always wanted BETTER!
Remember, everyone has a past and a story.
Take that pain and turn it into purpose,
believe beyond the betrayal and
know when failure comes your way stand on faith.

Last but not least,
remember who you are!
You are ENOUGH and you are WORTH IT!

Lee Davis Da Champ

Facebook: Elicah Mason
Instagram: @divas_by_faith_
Email: Divasbyfaithnotbysight@gmail.com

I am grateful for the truth of my intuition, for my anxiety is a lie.
I believe the divinity of my conscientiousness.
I respect my unfailing resilience.
I welcome the humanity of my vulnerability.

Jo Palmer
Instagram: @jpalm126

Life is easy if we understand that
we are not in control.
God's going to lay it out there for us
and we need to follow his lead.
Also, remember—love is the key!

Maxine McCullum-Gibson

You must love yourself before you can attempt to love anyone else.
Confidence is something you must have within yourself.
Without it, it's hard to believe in yourself.
With confidence, you will feel strength and it will help you in all
areas of life. As it relates to romantic relationships,
never be pushed into something that you don't want.
I guess the bottom line is, "know your worth."
Most of all keep God first and allow him to direct you.
Stay focused on him no matter what.

Pamela Caldwell

Follow your heart, that's where your passion lies. We always try to take the easy and most comfortable road, but that will only lead to a void you'll always try to fill. But when you follow your heart, it will lead to an uncompromising joy and a lifetime of happiness.

Don't let your failures overtake you.
Remember with great success comes several failures.
Pick yourself up,
brush yourself off,
and keep pushing forward.

Jackie Redic

Whatever you do, keep your mind focused on your goals and striving to make your life better. Discipline yourself.
Be good to yourself first and have it no other way.

Confidence to me comes from the word of God,
"I can do all things through Christ who strengthens me."
Surround yourself with people who love you.
Do not be afraid to say things you don't know so people can help you.
We are all different.
Confidence is embracing what makes you different,
accepting who you are, and sticking to it no matter what!

Connie French

You were created for a purpose.
Embrace the skin you're in and
surround yourself with positivity.
Block out the hate and be great.
Walk with confidence and keep the faith.
God has extraordinary plans for you.
Keep shining.

Whitney Taylor Ray
The Worldwide Whitness
Instagram: @WhitneyTaylorRay

Don't be afraid to admit to days when you feel weak or days you feel strong.

Seek encouragement when you feel weak and encourage others when you feel strong.

You have to give yourself the gratitude and appreciation for how far you have come so you don't miss the blessings right in front of you.

Trenea Baugh
Instagram: @trenea_m_b
Instagram: @nea_andherstyles

Embrace your obstacles, because they always lead you to the place you're supposed to be.
Follow that burning desire within, it'll help free your soul.

The visions and dreams you see, every day and night, are God's way of showing you your potential future.
He wouldn't allow you to envision something you couldn't have.

Ashley Lancaster
Instagram: @misslancaster
Instagram: @chasendreamsorg

Dear Beautiful Black Woman, YES!

Dear beautiful black woman, yes!
From the moment you open your eyes to moment you lay your crown down to sleep, sister, know that you have a birth right by The Creator to be here. By nature, excellence is in you. Let each step you take be a golden thread of pure brilliance and beauty.

Yes beauty, a word that perfectly describes you in all you are.
A synonym to your nature!
You are an influencer to many little black girls looking up to you. As you tread the paths walked by our loving mothers, you are creating a clearer path for those to follow after you, so, sister, walk with pride, dignity, and grace.

Yes grace, the warmth of your heart that holds a million sisters with love.
You are powerful! You are a force that creates change and shakes the norms. A force that liberates enslaved minds and moves boundaries. Your courage leaves trademarks of inspiration and strength.

Yes strength, the bravery of your soul that keeps those around you secure.
From the moment you open your eyes to the moment you lay your crown down to sleep, beautiful black woman, always remember that yes!
Yes, you are beauty, grace and strength.

Grace Zichawo (Zimbabwe)
Instagram: @gracebeautychic

Don't stop pursuing your dreams because you feel you aren't getting the support and love you deserve from others.
SHINE anyway!
You, your heart, your mission, and your goals
WILL move mountains and be successful!

De' Ashley Porterie

Strong, to me, means you acknowledge your emotions.

You're aware of the emotional trauma you're experiencing, lean into how you feel, and you work through your emotions, but you still move forward.

You can still pursue career opportunities, chase your personal goals, or make time for family and friends while you are healing.

Whatever you're experiencing can be discouraging but you ARE strong, and you WILL make it through.

Herbie Smith
Instagram: @missherbie

Situations where people don't care at all,
but you care too much,
can cause you a lot of stress.
Carrying on with this imbalance of care
is unfair to you and can be detrimental.

Do not allow people to change you or
completely turn off things you care about.
Get yourself together and focus on you.
Come up with a plan that allows you to care,
but in a way that is healthy for you.

Pia Grizzle

Know yourself and don't seek to be anything other than the beautiful queen you are.
Be a leader and not a follower, your journey is yours alone.
Every day is a new opportunity to define the woman you want to be.
Be charitable and find ways to inspire and share knowledge with others.

Hawa

In Genesis 9, God sealed His promise with a rainbow in the sky. In the midst of the devastation from the flood of judgment, there was a beautiful rainbow in the sky symbolizing God's gracious promise! But God's promise doesn't just show up after natural storms, sometimes His promise shows up after spiritual storms, too! My favorite scripture says, "For I know the plans I have for you," declares the Lord "plans to prosper you and not to harm you, plans to give you hope and a future." Jeremiah 29:11.

I have learned that our plan for our life is never God's plan. Therefore, when faced with hardships and affliction I encourage you to keep the faith. God did not promise we will never experience storms or reveal a timeline of when the storm will end. But He did promise He will be with us throughout the storm. For in a time of need and defeat, when you call the Lord, He will lift you up and make His plan clear.

Be encouraged, keep the faith, and He'll keep his promise.

La Shay Davis, M.S.
Instagram:@ExceptionalBarrierBreaker
Facebook: Exceptional Barrier Breaker
Email:ExceptionalBarrierBreaker@gmail.com

There are times where we acquiesce.
We know it's not right or
we know that thing or someone has not
met our standards, or our expectations and we adjust,
we bend, we make allowances.
We accept it.

But I say this to you.
Do not be afraid to stand up for your standards.
You will be happier for it. You'll be at peace.
Only accept things that serve the good in you.
Only take the best.
You are worth it. You are special. You are loved.

Love,

Amina S Hassan
Instagram: @Minzarella

Dear heart,

Breathe in the beauty of your skin.
Rub in some moisture and see how it glows.
Brown copper sunshine radiates from you,
you generate the energy of Mother Earth and
Mother Earth grows from your feet.
Weave flowers in your coils and
wreaths of leaves between your fingers.
You are the heart of all of us and we are the heart of you.

Love,

Fatima
Instagram: @foofoodays

Advice for My Sisters-in-Love
By Doris Session Gill

Put God first in your life. Lean on Him in every situation. Learn from Him.

Value yourself, your mind, and your body. Do not allow others to define your worth or tell you that you are not worthy of their respect or their best treatment. Love yourself enough to stand up for yourself. You are your first line of defense. Love yourself!! Don't let anyone cheapen you. That includes you. Eating healthy matters. You may live longer with greater mobility.

Do not expect others to fill any void or weak areas of your life. Others cannot make you happy. You are in control of that department.

Establish a pattern of saving your money on a regular and consistent basis. Save beyond your 401K. You may need some money that you don't want to be penalized for using.

Keep good credit. Pay your bills on time.

If you are a young mother, nurture your children. Don't expect TV, the Internet, relatives, or friends to raise them for you. You may not like what you get. Stand for what is right in the eyes and ears of your children. Let them see and hear you "doing the right thing." You are their first and foremost role model. If you are married, love your spouse and work with them towards your common goals.

Read your Bible. Don't let it decorate your end table in the closed position.

Pray without ceasing. In good times, as well as the bad. Prayer works!

Let the joy of the Lord be your strength. We cannot handle this world alone. The haters are too clever, and they don't let up. Trust in the Lord and take yourself to church on a regular basis.

Believe this... God LOVES you anyway! He forgives you in spite of! Enjoy your life. Make the most of your life. It's the only one you have.

I wish someone affirmed the importance of loving myself through the highs and the lows and the thick and thin of life.
Remember through it all, love on you and what's for you is exclusively yours.

Rayneshia James (Rahsunn)
Instagram: @Chakrahz
Facebook: @RahsCo
Website: rahshandcraftedsoapandscrubs.org

You are not crazy or broken.
You are experiencing a sane and rational response to broken situations.

Luke 6:41 "Why do you look at the speck of sawdust in your brother's eye and pay no attention to the plank in your own eye?"

Never miss a chance to make a good memory.

Bryoney Hayes
Instagram: @b_averial
Email: bryoneyh@gmail.com
Website: postagestamprequired.Wordpress.com

"For You formed my innermost parts; You knit me in my mother's womb. I will give thanks and praise to You, for I am fearfully and wonderfully made; Wonderful are Your works, and my soul knows it very well." Psalms 139: 13-14

You are fearfully and wonderfully made! You are a unique creation, built with great reverence, heart-felt interest, and respect, from the start. There is no one like you, so revel in it! You have a purpose, so find it and live it!

You are a magnificent masterpiece, a work of God; so know your value!

Keep your eyes on the prize

Don't get distracted from what it is you want to accomplish. There will be a lot of distractions that will hinder your progress towards the goals that you set for yourself. Watch out for them; don't get caught up and lost. Remember the prize and stay focused!

There is blessing in being corrected

No one likes being corrected, critiqued, criticized, or told that you didn't do as well as you thought. After all, you are a masterpiece! But the truth is that to be a G.O.A.T., you must go through growing pains. And growing is a blessing. Learn from your mistakes, listen to those that have traveled the roads you are on, and respect those in authority (they have a wealth of information that you cannot find in college books). Be willing to accept that you may not know everything. And never ever stop learning!

For corn to grow, rain must fall

There will be rain on your journey. Life is not fair and it's not easy. Accept that fact. Things or plans will not go as you want. People will disappoint you and hurt you. You will fall. You will FAIL. Life will get you down and make you want to give up. But, it's the RAIN that will cause you to pull yourself up and rise above it all to a new level of greatness.

Giving up is never an option
This is one of the great mantras that my dear mother often told me. Don't give up. You may have to take a break, take a deep breath, scratch your head, pray, eat a pint of ice cream with cookies—whatever it takes. But under no circumstances will we give up! Keep fighting the fight; it is worth it in the end. You can do it.

Anchor Yourself
Be very sure your anchor holds and grips a solid rock. Not to sound too "churchy," but that rock is Jesus! That's another "pearl of wisdom" from my mother. In this journey of life, you will need to have a solid foundation that will give you peace, focus, and comfort your spirit.

Deirdre Delcambre-Thigpen, M.S., M.Ed., CCC-SLP
Email: ddtslp@gmail.com

When you're going through turmoil and you start to lose hope,
please know that God has the master plan.
So, when you don't know what to do, let go and let God.
He'll reveal your plan when he deems you ready.

Gloria Stevens

Beautiful Queen,

I know you are strong.

I see it in the way you beat the odds.

I see it in the way you give when you are most in need.

I'm thankful for you and just know that you inspire me every day.

Lynn Jouini

Instagram: @Itsthelynn

A Word for a Strong Black Woman

Dear Strong Black Woman,

Every effort you put in, though society may turn a blind eye, does not go unnoticed. Our hard work continues to turn heads and change lives, and the world reaps the benefits of the seeds that we sow.

We are the blueprint, the foundation, the rock. We are what keeps the world turning. While the world puts us in a box and tells us we are only good for certain things, we continue to break the mold. We never stop. We, black women, are placed at the bottom, but we continue to rise to the top.

Never forget that you are a child of the Most High, forged in sunlight and dipped in ebony. Truly a masterpiece, and a fire that the world will never tame. This is a truth you mustn't forget.

Go and continue to change the world because, without you— without us—there wouldn't be a world to change.

Yours,
JaNay Redic
Instagram: @nayredphoto

Put God first in everything you do—when things are going well, not so well—even when you feel He's not present.
It is in those times that He is testing your faith—trust in Him.

Eagles do not hang around with chickens!
Surround yourself with like-minded individuals. Be careful with whom you share your dreams—not everyone is on your side.

Develop a mantra or chose a
favorite scripture to recite daily to keep you inspired.
Write your goals, dreams, and visions down where you can see them each day. Let this serve as motivation, as well as a gauge to track your progress. Plan your work, then work your plan.

Do not focus on where you are, nor what you have. Focus on who you want to become. God has equipped you with everything you need to succeed!

Laureen F. Holmes
Facebook: Just Me Catering
Email: 07bosslady07@gmail.com

Always go with your first mind and do not second guess yourself. Trust your thoughts, emotions, and intuition.

Constance French

You celebrate that new job, passing a major exam, launching your business, getting a promotion, and all major accomplishments in your life.

You treat yourself because you have worked hard for these accomplishments, but what do you deserve for the things you do every day?

Do you view these things as nothing special?

Don't forget to celebrate being a bad ass every day.
Too often you minimize the daily tasks you demolish.
Celebrate crossing-off things on your to-do list,
celebrate the dedication to studying for the exam,
celebrate the daily magic you create at your job or business.
Celebrate and treat yourself for being a top-tier queen!

Aarion Josey

Don't worry about walking away from things you once prayed for if you are not in a respected space.
You deserve to be treated with the highest level of respect.
Walk away with your head held high and know that the right opportunities will present themselves to you.

Lee Waters

Protect your positive energy at all costs.

Don't allow anyone, friends and family included, to drain you of that energy.

Disconnect and isolate when necessary, and don't feel guilty about it.

You are allowed to put yourself first and focus on your own well-being.

Keleigh Kyle
Instagram: @kustomkreated

Dear sis,

You are magical as fuck!

Everything you touch turns to gold!

The universe is always working in your favor in ALL WAYS.

Sit back on your throne like the beautiful goddess you are!

You don't chase the bag, the bag chases you!

I love you and remember you are enough, and

YOU ARE WORTHY!

PERIOD!!!

KayLove

Instagram: @nailkhemistry

Facebook: Nail Khemistry by Kay

Dear Black Queens,
We work better under pressure!
When life throws a curve-ball don't be a victim!
Pick yourself up and adjust your CROWN!

Embrace your weaknesses, they will only make you stronger.
Applaud your success, you deserve nothing but the best!
Most importantly,
love yourself for who you are!
We are beautiful, intelligent, articulate,
creative, fearless and, most of all, self-driven!
We are Black Queens!!

Demitra Thompson

Have the courage to say what needs to be said.
Your silence serves no one.
You may not think your ideas are good enough,
you may not think you are qualified or capable enough, or
you may worry about what others think.

But let me tell you something—
there are others in the room who are half as qualified,
half as knowledgeable, and half as good
who will speak up twice as much as anyone else.
Don't let their voice overshadow yours.

You may also be the person who speaks up for someone else
and you may not even realize it.
You don't know who is waiting for someone to take the lead...
so, you take the lead!
Be self-aware and recognize your impact but go ahead and say it.
Be honest, confident, and realistic about what you have to say.
Let your presence and your voice show up in the world.

Denise Balfour Simpson, PhD
Email: denise.balfour@gmail.com
Instagram: @dsimps04

Find yourself.
She can ALWAYS be found.
She is right there in your mind, body, and soul.
She's in your thoughts, your behaviors, and most importantly,
she is nestled right in the very core of your heart.
Yearn for her!
Desire self-love and self-compassion at the same levels
that you offer that same love and compassion to others.
Now, once you find her,
find your tribe,
then thrive.

Dr. Amy S. Walker, Licensed Psychologist
Email: ascwalker@gmail.com

In life, no matter what age, never consider yourself a failure. You only fail when you don't at least try. Remember, nothing in life is easy, so never give up. The first attempt may not work in your favor but keep going.

LaQuiesha Caldwell
Email: laquiesharaychelle@gmail.com

Be patient with yourself, you will change like every season.

Set weekly goals for yourself to provide motivation.

Don't believe everything people tell you. Go off people's actions.

Don't fall in love with someone's potential; you will be waiting forever.

Never compromise your self-value for anyone
because this world is everyone for themselves.

Don't be too hard on yourself you're human—you will make mistakes.

If you notice yourself with the same end results with all of your relationships, you have to be the person to make the change. Notice the pattern.

Don't overlook your intuition—that's God's way of talking to you.

Bianca Kostack

Growing up, my role models were the older women in my family. Their resilience, strength, and astuteness are admirable traits that were passed down to me. For example, the greatest thing I learned, from my late grandmother, is the importance of giving others grace and space to change for the better. I believe we are all a constant work-in-progress with the ability to grow towards a positive trajectory.

Jaime LaDawn Roya
Instagram: @jai_ladawn

Queen love on yourself hard core! I understand we all have insecurities, flaws, and we are our worst critics. You want the very best for yourself and there is nothing wrong with that. You cannot get to the best without going through good and better. You have to love who you were, who you are, and who you want to be.

When I say you are the universe, I mean it! Do not let anyone, including yourself, reduce your magic. Do not let people manipulate you with bare minimum rewards when you are giving maximum effort. This goes for your job, partner/spouse, and friends.

Make notes, create black women "universe" accountability groups, and tell yourself every day you are amazing. Turn to your community of love and seek resources of support. I can definitely hear my friends saying "aht aht…you're speaking that basic Earth shit, Fe!" Awareness of your magic can help you shift your circumstances.

Live the most beautiful life you can. Trust me, I know life is not always kind. The good times are lovely, but the bad times are painful. When times are good, revel in these moments. Be sure to store them in your "life is good" memory space because you will need them when bad times creep in.

When I tell you anything is possible, I mean it. Look at the opportunities of 2021. Twenty years ago, no one encouraged us to be social media managers, marketing strategists, influencers, or vloggers but these jobs exist today. You are more than capable of doing and being anything you want. You have to lead with confidence. When you are on the brink of greatness, doubt will creep in to test your confidence. If doubt wins, you cannot reach your full potential. Kick doubt's ass, the world is yours!

I love you,
Phylicia French

THANK YOU, SIS

To the beautiful black woman reading this,

I want to thank you for reading my labor my love. If you have made it to this page, I know you have been encouraged, inspired, and received great advice from my community of phenomenal black women.

The advice and words of encouragement from the women in this book are golden! To the beautiful women that contributed to this book, and every black woman that has poured love and positivity into me, I thank you, I love you, and I am so blessed to have crossed paths with you.

Being a black woman is so powerful, so magical, so special, and so spiritual. Remember, you have all the answers within, sis. I wish you nothing but magic, love in abundance, and your definition of success.

Visit phyliciafrench.com to continue your transformative breakthrough journey with me. Follow me on social media to join the universe sisterhood!

Instagram: @sisyouaretheuniverse
Instagram: @phyliciafrench
Facebook: Sis, You Are the Universe

Remember, you are the universe!

With a full heart of love,
Phylicia French

Made in the USA
Columbia, SC
26 April 2021

36945585R00109